THE

SURRENDER

NOVENA A

POWERFUL

PRAYER BOOK

TO COME

BEFORE GOD

CONTENT

INTRODUCTION

The Surrender Novena is a profound and transformative spiritual trip that beckons us to release the burdens of our lives into the hands of Divine Providence. embedded in the training of Jesus Christ and inspired by the wisdom of Saint Padre Pio, this novena is a testament to the extraordinary power of surrendering to God's will.

In a world frequently marked by stress, query, and the grim pursuit of control, the Surrender Novena offers solace and guidance. It teaches us to relinquish our fears, anxieties, and solicitations, placing our trust in a advanced plan far wiser than our own.

Over the course of nine days, you'll embark on a trip of tone-discovery and spiritual growth. Each day, we will explore different aspects of rendition, allowing you to let go of what weighs you down and to open your heart to the divine love that awaits.

As you embark on this novena, may you find peace in rendition, strength in trust, and the profound joy of aligning your will with God's. Through this novena, you'll come to understand that true freedom lies in surrendering to the One who knows your heart's deepest solicitations and who always works for your ultimate good.

Prepare to embark on a spiritual adventure as we claw into the Surrender Novena, and may your trip be filled with grace, blessings, and a deeper connection to the bottomless love of our Creator.

Let us begin this transformative trip with an open heart and a amenability to surrender.

THE HISTORY OF THE SURRENDER NOVENA

Saint Padre Pio St. Pio of Pietrelcina was an Italian Capuchin friar who lived in the 20th century. He was famed for his deep church, holiness, and the smirches (injuries of Christ) that he bore on his body. Padre Pio was known for his unwavering trust in God's providence and his stimulant of others to surrender to God's will.

Alleviation for the Novena The Surrender Novena was born out of Padre Pio's training and guidance to his spiritual children. He frequently emphasized the significance of surrendering one's life to God and trusting in His plan. The novena is a structured way to exercise this rendition and grow in faith.

Nine Days of Surrender The novena consists of a nine- day prayer sequence, where each day focuses on surrendering a specific aspect of one's life or enterprises to God. The novena culminates in total rendition on the ninth day, trusting God fully.

Spread of the Novena The practice of the Surrender Novena gained fashionability through the jottings and training of Padre Pio. His spiritual wisdom and guidance were extensively participated, and numerous people began incorporating the novena into their diurnal spiritual routines.

Continued Influence Indeed after Padre Pio's end in 1968, the Surrender Novena continues to be a cherished and important spiritual practice for numerous individualities seeking to consolidate their faith and trust in God.

moment, the Surrender Novena is rehearsed by people of colorful religious backgrounds as a means of chancing peace, hope, and solace in surrendering their enterprises and worries to a advanced power. It remains a testament to the enduring impact of Saint Padre Pio's church and his emphasis on surrendering to God's loving providence.

HOW TO PRAY THE NOVENA

Day 1: Surrendering Our Lives

Begin with the Sign of the Cross.

Reflect on the aspect of your life you want to surrender to God's will.

Recite the opening prayer for the novena.

Say the prayer for Day 1, surrendering your life to God.

Conclude with your personal intentions or prayers.

Days 2-8: Specific Surrenders
the sign of Cross

Reflect on the specific aspect mentioned for that day (e.g., worries, desires, relationships).

Recite the opening prayer for the novena.

Say the prayer for that particular day's surrender.

Conclude with your personal intentions or prayers.

Day 9: Total Surrender

Begin with the Sign of the Cross.

Reflect on your willingness to surrender everything to God.

Recite the opening prayer for the novena.

Say the prayer for Day 9, which is about total surrender.

Conclude with your personal intentions or prayers.

Closing Prayer:

After completing the Day 9 prayer, say a closing prayer to conclude the novena.

Thank God for His love and grace throughout the nine days.

Tips:

Find a quiet, peaceful place to pray.

Focus on each day's specific surrender and trust in God's plan.

Be sincere and open in your prayers, pouring out your heart to God.

You can keep a journal to record your thoughts, reflections, and any insights during the novena.

Remember that the Surrender Novena is not just about reciting words but also about cultivating a deep trust in God's providence and surrendering your concerns to Him. It's a personal and profound spiritual journey that can bring peace and clarity to your life as you learn to let go and trust in God's plan.

NOVENA
PRAYERS

DAY 1
SURRENDERING OUR LIVES

Opening Prayer

Do the sign of Cross

Dear Lord Jesus Christ, I come before you moment with an open heart, Ready to surrender my life to your divine will. You're the author of my life, my purpose, and my fortune. I trust in your loving plan for me, And I offer my entire being to your guidance.

Prayer for Day 1 Heavenly Father, I surrender my life into your hands. You know me better than I know myself. You know my expedients, my dreams, my fears, and my dubieties. I trust that you have a beautiful plan for me, Indeed when I can not see it easily.

Help me, Lord, to follow your path with faith and modesty. Guide me in every decision I make, So that I may live a life pleasing to you. I let go of my own solicitations and intentions, And I place my life entirely in your loving care.

I surrender, Lord, all that I'm and all that I have, For I know that your will is always perfect. Fill me with your grace and peace, As I walk this trip of rendition. May your divine wisdom light my way, And may I find my true purpose in serving you.

I make this rendition with a thankful heart, Trusting that your love for me knows no bounds. In the name of Jesus, I supplicate. Amen.

ending Prayer

Do the sign of Cross

DAY 2
SURRENDERING OUR WORRIES

Opening Prayer

Do the sign of Cross

Dear Heavenly Father, As I embark on this alternate day of the Surrender Novena, I come before you with a heart burdened by worries and anxieties. I know that you're the source of all peace, And I trust that I can surrender my enterprises to you.

Prayer for Day 2 Loving God, moment, I offer up to you all my worries and anxieties. You know the troubles that weigh heavy on my heart, The fears that keep me awake at night, And the misgivings that cloud my mind.

I surrender these worries to you, Lord, For I know that you're my retreat and strength. Help me to release my grip on these enterprises, And to place my trust entirely in your hands.

Educate me to have faith in your godly providence, To believe that you're working for my good, Indeed in the midst of life's challenges. Grant me the serenity to accept what I can not change, The courage to change what I can, And the wisdom to discern the difference.

I choose to cast my cares upon you, Lord, For you watch for me with an horizonless love. Fill my heart with your peace and assurance, Knowing that you're in control of all effects.

I surrender my worries to you, O God, And I place my stopgap in your unerring grace.

ending Prayer
Do the sign of Cross

DAY 3
SURRENDERING OUR DESIRES

Opening Prayer
Do the sign of Cross

Dear Heavenly Father, As I continue this Surrender Novena, I come before you with a heart filled with desires and bournes . Help me to surrender these desires to your loving will.

Prayer for Day 3 Loving God, moment, I lay before you my deepest desires and dreams. You know the jones of my heart, The pretensions and intentions I hold dear, And the paths I wish to follow.

I surrender these desires to you, Lord, For I trust that your plan for me is lesser than my own. Help me to relinquish any attachment to specific issues, And to be open to the paths you have prepared for me.

entitlement me the wisdom to discern your will, And the courage to follow it faithfully. May your desires become my desires, And may I find joy and fulfillment in aligning my life with your purpose.

I place my trust in your providence, O God, Knowing that you'll lead me to where I need to be. Fill me with your peace as I surrender my desires, And help me to accept your perfect plan with gratefulness.

I surrender my desires into your loving hands, Lord, And I await your guidance with an open heart.

ending Prayer
Do the sign of Cross

Opening Prayer
Do the sign of Cross

Dear Heavenly Father, As I continue this Surrender Novena, I come before you with my relationships, both cherished and challenged. I surrender them to your wisdom and love.

Prayer for Day 4 Loving God, moment, I surrender to you all my connections — My family, musketeers, loved bones , and those with whom I may struggle. You know the mannas and sorrows within these bonds, The love and forgiveness they may bear, And the mending that may be demanded.

I lay these relationships at your bases, Lord, For I trust that you hold the key to harmony and reconciliation. Help me to let go of any resentments or grievances, And to open my heart to forgiveness and understanding.

Grant me the strength to nurture and appreciate the positive connections, And the tolerance to mend and heal the simulated ones. May your love be the foundation of all my connections, And may I be an instrument of your peace and love in their lives.

I surrender my relationships into your hands, O God, And I ask for your guidance in fostering bonds of love and concinnity. Fill my heart with your compassion and grace, As I entrust these precious connections to your care.

ending Prayer
Do the sign of Cross

DAY 5
SURRENDERING OUR FAILURES

Opening Prayer

Do the sign of Cross

Dear Heavenly Father, As I continue this Surrender Novena, I come before you with modesty, admitting my failures. I surrender them to your mercy and guidance.

Prayer for Day 5 Merciful God, moment, I bring ahead you my failures and failings. I fete the times when I've fallen short of your prospects, When I've made miscalculations, and when I've let myself and others down.

I surrender these failures to you, Lord, For I know that you're a God of forgiveness and redemption. Help me to release the burden of guilt and self- criticism, And to accept your loving forgiveness.

entitlement me the grace to learn from my failures, To grow stronger in my faith and character, And to use these gests to come a better person.

I trust that you can bring good indeed out of my mistakes, And I surrender my once failures into your hands, O God.

Fill me with your love, mercy, and the courage to move forward, Knowing that your grace is sufficient for me.

ending Prayer
Do the sign of Cross

DAY 6
SURRENDERING OUR UNBORN

Dear Heavenly Father, As I continue this Surrender Novena, I come before you with query about my future. I surrender it to your divine plan and providence.

Prayer for Day 6 Gracious God, moment, I offer up to you my expedients and fears about the future. You know the dreams and intentions I hold, The unknown paths that lie ahead, And the questions that keep me awake at night.

I surrender my future to you, Lord, For I trust that you hold the map of my life's trip. Help me to release my anxiety about what lies ahead, And to place my confidence in your loving guidance.

entitlement me the wisdom to discern your will for my future, And the courage to follow your path with faith. May your plans come my plans, And may I find peace in knowing that you're with me every step of the way.

I trust in your providence, O God, And I surrender my future into your hands. Fill me with hope and assurance as I embrace the unknown, For I know that you're the author of my story.

ending Prayer
Do the sign of Cross

DAY 7
SURRENDERING OUR HEALTH

Opening Prayer

Do the sign of Cross

Dear Heavenly Father, As I continue this Surrender Novena, I come before you with enterprises about my health. I surrender it to your mending grace and wisdom.

Prayer for Day 7 Healing God, moment, I offer up to you my physical and internal health. You know the challenges I face, The illnesses that affect me, and the pain I may endure.

I surrender my health to you, Lord, For I trust in your power to heal and restore. Grant me the strength to endure any trials or suffering, And the tolerance to accept my limitations.

May your healing touch be upon me, And may I find comfort in your presence during times of illness. I trust in your plan for my well- being, And I surrender my health into your able hands.

Fill me with hope, adaptability, and gratefulness, As I trip through the ups and downs of health. May your mending grace be a source of strength and renewal.

ending Prayer
Do the sign of Cross

DAY 8
SURRENDERING OUR WEALTH

Opening Prayer

Do the sign of Cross

Dear Heavenly Father, As I continue this Surrender Novena, I come before you with my wealth and material effects. I surrender them to your providence and liberality.

Prayer for Day 8 Generous God, moment, I offer up to you all that I retain — My wealth, effects, and material cornucopia. You know the blessings and coffers I have, And the ways in which I can partake them with others.

I surrender my wealth to you, Lord, For I trust that you're the source of all cornucopia. Help me to be a faithful slavey of what you have entrusted to me, And to use my coffers for the good of others and your area.

Grant me a generous heart, O God, And help me to partake with those in need. May I be a conduit of your love and compassion in the world, And may I find true richness in acts of kindness and liberality.

I trust in your providence, knowing that you give for all our needs. I surrender my wealth into your hands, And I ask for the wisdom to use it wisely and for your glory.

ending Prayer
Do the sign of Cross

DAY 9
TOTAL SURRENDER

Opening Prayer

Do the sign of Cross

Dear Heavenly Father, As I reach the final day of this Surrender Novena, I come before you with a heart open and willing to surrender everything. I place my total trust in your loving and fortuitous care.

Prayer for Day 9 Loving and Merciful God, moment, I stand before you with complete rendition. I offer you every aspect of my life — My history, present, and future, My mannas and sorrows, My strengths and sins, My expedients and fears, My effects and connections, And every desire of my heart.

I surrender it all, Lord, for I trust in your horizonless wisdom and love. I admit that your plan for me is far lesser than my own. Help me to let go of any attachments and control, And to accept your divine will with gratitude and humility.

Grant me the grace to follow you faithfully, No matter where your path may lead. May my life be a living testament to your love and grace.

I surrender, Lord, not out of weakness, but out of strength, For in rendition, I find true freedom and peace. May your will be done in me and through me, And may I always seek to glorify your name.

I place my total surrender into your loving hands, O God, And I trust that you'll guide me on the trip of faith.

ending Prayer
Do the sign of Cross

Conclusion

As we conclude this transformative trip through the Surrender Novena, we're reminded of the profound beauty and power of surrendering our lives to God. Over the course of these nine days, we've explored colorful facets of rendition — our lives, worries, solicitations, connections, failures, future, health, wealth, and, eventually, our total rendition. Through prayer and reflection, we've drawn near to the heart of God, learning to trust in His godly providence.

Surrender isn't a sign of weakness but a demonstration of our faith and trust in God's perfect plan. It's an act of courage, a amenability to let go of our own limited understanding and embrace His measureless wisdom. In rendition, we find peace, strength, and freedom, for we release the burdens that weigh us down and place them into the hands of the One who can carry them with ease.

As we move forward from this novena, let us carry the spirit of rendition with us in our diurnal lives. May we remember that rendition isn't a one- time event but a nonstop trip of trust and reliance on God. In moments of uncertainty, fear, or doubt, may we return to the assignments learned then, knowing that we can surrender all into His loving care.

We express our gratefulness for the opportunity to embark on this novena together and for the grace that flows from rendition. May the Surrender Novena continue to be a source of strength, hope, and transformation in your life. And may you always find comfort in the words of Jesus" Come to me, all you who are sick and burdened, and I'll give you rest "(Matthew 11:28).

May God's love and peace accompany you on your trip of rendition, and may His will be your guiding light now and always.

You can write down your wish here